## TEEN EDITION
# Diamond in the Rough

# TEEN EDITION
# Diamond in the Rough

## SHALORIA MITCHELL

Diamond in the Rough – Teen Edition
Published by Purposely Created Publishing Group
Copyright © 2017 Shaloria Mitchell

All rights reserved. No part of this book may be reproduced, distributed or transmitted in any form by any means, graphics, electronics, or mechanical, including photocopy, recording, taping, or by any information storage or retrieval system, without permission in writing from the publisher, except in the case of reprints in the context of reviews, quotes, or references.

Scripture quotations marked (NKJV) are taken from the New King James Version ® Copyright © 1982 by Thomas Nelson, Inc. All rights reserved.

Scriptures marked MSG are taken from The Message®. Copyright © 1993, 1994, 1995, 1996, 2000, 2001, 2002. Used by permission of NavPress Publishing Group.

Published by: Purposely Created Publishing Group™

Author photo taken by: Juanita Toronto

Printed in the United States of America

ISBN-13: 978-1-945558-51-1

---

Special discounts are available on bulk quantity purchases by book clubs, associations, and special interest groups. For details email:
Sales@PublishYourGift.com or call (866) 674-3340.

**For more information, log onto**
www.PublishYourGift.com

# Dedicated To You

This book is dedicated to my young ladies.

Never become defeated.

It will all work out together for you. Don't give up.
The best will soon shine through. Just understand that
you are beautifully created.

*And we know that all things work together for good to
those who love God, to those who are the called
according to His purpose.* —Romans 8:28

# Table of Contents

| | | |
|---|---|---|
| Acknowledgments | | ix |
| Poem | | xiii |
| Preface | | xv |
| Introduction | Diamonds | 1 |
| Chapter 1 | The Making of a Diamond | 5 |
| Chapter 2 | The Diamond Cutting Process | 15 |
| Chapter 3 | Planning Stage | 25 |
| Chapter 4 | Maximizing Value | 31 |
| Chapter 5 | Weight Retention | 37 |
| Chapter 6 | Color Retention | 43 |
| Chapter 7 | Maximization Turnaround Stage | 49 |
| Chapter 8 | Cleaving Stage | 57 |
| Chapter 9 | Bruting Stage | 65 |
| Chapter 10 | Polishing Process | 71 |
| Chapter 11 | The Final Inspection | 75 |
| Chapter 12 | The Carat, Cut, Color, and Clarity of the Diamond | 81 |
| About the Author | | 87 |

# Acknowledgments

What a mighty God we serve!

I just want to give honor to my sweet savior Jesus Christ (Yahshua). God (Yahweh), He is everything, and without Him I am nothing.

When no one else was there, He was right by my side through the good and bad. God continuously shows me unconditional love, favor, grace, and mercy.

No doubt about it, I would be silly not to serve such a wonderful king, who is so selfless that He gave His only son that I may have life eternally. I am truly blessed.

Thank you God (Yahweh), you are an amazing father, teacher, and friend in my life.

Thank you Jesus (Yahshua), you gave your life for my sins: past, present, and future.

*To my beautiful children:*

Gemaryah – Baby girl, we have been through some things. I know you took on the mommy role in my selfish acts. I admire the lady you are. You are a rare pearl, who I appreciate and love. You have stuck it out with me through thick and thin. I will forever have a great bond with you, my princess.

Joshua and Jaden – my princes, my protectors, and my gentlemen, I appreciate you for watching over mommy, for your prayers, letters, and cries to God. You both have touched me dearly. What would I do without my men?

Obviance – Your laughter keeps me alive. You are my sunshine in the middle of the storm. You came at a time when all hope was gone, but God knew just who to send.

My angels, Gemayah, Joshua, Jaden, and Obviance – You have loved me even when I did not love myself. When I did not know how to be a mother, in my own selfishness, you never judged me, and you still showed me respect and love, even in my wrongdoing.

Thank you for allowing God to reshape, remake, and remold me all over again! I love you guys so much! You are so precious to me! I know that each one of you is a special gift from God. I remember that old saying, "It takes a village to raise a child." I consider myself to be that child. It took those special people that God appointed in my life: my children, my beautiful mother, some family, extended family, friends, pastors, church family, teachers, and just everyone that God allowed in my life, whether for a season or a lifetime.

To my biggest fans (the haters and enemies) - I would not have been able to do this without you. You guys helped me to have one of the best relationships with God because you kept me in His face. I thank you all. I appreciate you for bringing me to a place of maturity through lessons, encouraging words, discipline, and motivation. I love you all dearly.

RIH, my angels:

Delilah "Auntie Dee" Mitchell, Rachael T. Yahsha, and Cleola Mitchell.

# Our Deepest Fear

*By Marianne Williamson*

Our deepest fear is not that we are inadequate; our deepest fear is that we are powerful beyond measure. It is our light, not our darkness that frightens us.

We ask ourselves, "Who am I to be brilliant, gorgeous, talented, and fabulous?" Actually, who are you *not* to be? You are a child of God. Playing small does not serve the world. There is nothing enlightening about shrinking so that other people won't feel insecure around you. We are all meant to shine as children do. We were born of God, who is within us. It is in everyone. And as we let our light shine, we unconsciously give other people permission to do the same. As we are liberated from our own fear, our presence automatically liberates others.

# Preface

Every situation, mistake, and failure has been used to make and mold me. I am not perfect, but I am definitely not the woman I used to be. I was inspired to write this book for all whom have ever felt rejected or have had people look over you, leaving you to think that you were nothing.

I am here to encourage you by sharing some of my personal experiences, mistakes, disappointments, failures, and heartaches—the things no one wants to talk about when they feel they have arrived. *Those things!* No need to be ashamed. There are people going through some of the same things, whether they admit it or not. I want to be a voice, in hopes that it will release a chain reaction for us all to be helpers to one another. Who knows? Your story could help me!

I was a fatherless, teen mother. A victim of abuse—sexually, emotionally, and physically. I even wanted to commit suicide at one point. I have abused alcohol, as well as sex. I've lied, cheated, stolen, and have lost very important friends and family to death. I am not glorifying what I used to do. I just want you to see that you are not alone. You can overcome and make it through your process. I am not that person to hide behind a mask. I share all I've been through to let you know that I am just like you.

I want to share the "in between" stuff. The stuff that, when you think you have gotten a little successful, you want to turn your nose up at people and act as if you have never done anything. And when someone else messes up, you point your finger. Yeah, *that* stuff. Because all you see is the end result, how wonderful everything is now. Many are too afraid to admit where they came from, and what it took to make it out, to see the full manifestation of God's best work. Keep in mind that if God can turn me around and bless me, He most certainly can do the same thing for you. God loves you regardless of what you have done. Allow Jesus to be your savior and everything else you need Him to be. I know; I tried him for myself, and He's the only one who turned out to be faithful and true.

Just think: If you have done everything on your own and it has not worked yet, it will not hurt you to receive a little help from someone who loves you in spite of what you have done and will not throw it back in your face. God is someone who you can bring all your baggage to, to help you unload it without asking any questions or have any pre-judgments. We were created for a purpose—beautifully created, just the way God intended for us to be.

Beautifully created means that God created you with sincere effort that delights Him, meaning He is excited that He brought you into existence. And you were wonderfully made with special instructions, to be handled with care. From this point on, know who you are and who you belong to.

*"Oh yes, you shaped me first inside, then out;*
  *you formed me in my mother's womb.*
*I thank you, High God—you're breathtaking!*
  *Body and soul, I am marvelously made!*
  *I worship in adoration—what a creation!*
*You know me inside and out,*
  *you know every bone in my body;*
*You know exactly how I was made, bit by bit,*
  *how I was sculpted from nothing into something.*
*Like an open book, you watched me grow from conception to birth;*
  *all the stages of my life were spread out before you,*
*The days of my life all prepared*
  *before I'd even lived one day."* – Psalm 139:13-16 (MSG)

You are beautiful just how God made you, and He loves us unconditionally—even with our jacked up selves. The beauty of it is that God loves to use the people you least expect, especially the ones no one would ever think of. God is amazing like that. He is always preparing a table in the presence of everyone who has doubted or talked about you. He is funny like that. And before you know it, your life will be turned upside down.

*"Before I shaped you in the womb,*
  *I knew all about you.*
*Before you saw the light of day,*
  *I had holy plans for you:*
*A prophet to the nations—*
  *that's what I had in mind for you."* – Jeremiah 1:5

You will find the true you, the person buried underneath it all, when going through life's journey. We make mistakes and deal with hurt, disappointments, hardships, embarrassments, failures, and heartaches. These all turn our focus away from the very reasons why they may occur in the first place. When these things happen, we allow them to build a front, a shield, a mask, or a cover-up to protect ourselves, and we don't allow the real us to shine through. We often lose sight of our true self, and we begin to believe all the lies and opinions of others. We allow those things inside our mind and they begin to take form.

This book is written to encourage you to continue through your process and not give up! To grow in your full potential in God so we can be used to help the next person. I want you to know that you are beautifully created, and fearfully and wonderfully made.

There can never be another you. Not everyone can go through what you have been through and make it out. You are unique and handpicked. From this day forward, do not believe another lie, and even if it was the truth…SO WHAT?! You were created to manifest the glory of God. God loves you so much so that He gave His only son to lay down His life for you.

*"For God so loved the world that He gave His only begotten Son, that whoever believes in Him should not perish but have everlasting life."* – John 3:16

There is no greater love than that. Embrace who you are and love yourself. Share your story in hopes that someone else will come out of what you already overcame. You never know who just might need to hear it.

# Introduction

## DIAMONDS

*"For she is more profitable than silver and yields better returns than gold." –* Proverbs 3:14

You are a diamond! You may not see yourself as one, but you are important and valuable. You were bought with the highest price. Diamonds are a beautiful and brilliant creation. Diamonds in the rough are found in various parts of the world and are often overlooked. Not even realizing the true beauty that it possesses, it seems as if no one is there for *us*; no one understands.

The outer layer, where we grow larger, is God separating us from the rest. The more you are under heat and pressure, the more beautifully valuable and defined you become. A diamond is UNBREAKABLE and does not fold under pressure. The more you endure, the larger you grow, the more polished you become, and the more you will shine through.

In 2 Corinthians 12, Paul talks about a thorn in his side causing severe pain and discomfort. Paul prayed for God to take it away. In turn, God gave him the revelation that even though the thorns hurt, they served a very useful purpose, preventing him from becoming prideful. Paul found it to be a good thing that God used to help him grow. Just look back and think what persons, things, and places in your life have caused you an uncomfortable, inexplicable feeling. Now look at those things as tools used to make and mold you. You are becoming a very valuable instrument to be used for Him by Him. I told you God is funny! From the Greek word, meaning "UNBREAKABLE," a diamond is:

- ◊ Long lasting and indestructible because it is made under extreme pressure, as well as extreme heat.

- ◊ Resistant, tough, and sturdy because it is made up of the hardest rock matter. They are heavy duty and last forever.

- ◊ Found deep in the earth's core. The longer the diamonds are there, the more they grow.

- ◊ Shatterproof. After a diamond is cut into the gem that it is selected to be, it then possesses a certain uniqueness and beauty that no one can figure out.

- ◊ Commands its own value once it has completed its process.

- ◊ Pleases the eye. The most important quality that a diamond has is beauty—its shape, color, and the way it is made. However, a diamond in the rough, which is its original state, is very different from the finished product and is not at all appealing.

- ◊ Treasured in such a way that people have actually killed to possess them. So much so that even cubic zirconia are often substituted. Though it's not a real diamond, cubic zirconia have more of an extreme heat and pressure to undergo.

# *One*

## THE MAKING OF A DIAMOND

*THE MAKING OF:*

_____

(Insert your name above)

Diamonds are found in the outer layer of the earth. The temperature during a volcano eruption causes a diamond rough to form into the hard rock that it is. Can you imagine the heat? This is how hot the temperature must be just to create the rough stone. Diamonds are measured on a Mohn's scale, which measures the hardness versus the weight. The diamond's hardness determines the purity and can only be damaged by another diamond. Similarly, we are made with the pressures of life and everything that comes along with it. We are judged by how well we can handle it. Some of our situations become very heated and may feel like we're under fire.

We allow ourselves to get frustrated by relationships with others, school, mistakes, failures, disappointments, our families and so on. We get caught up in people's opinions and responses regarding us and our circumstances. We have endured pain, hurt, embarrassment, fear, and different obstacles that come our way. We deal with things the best we know how, but God knows the right heat and pressure that we need to make us shine.

Some of my personal pressures were dealing with low self-esteem. I had no idea of my self-worth or anything I really had inside of me, and that left the door open for settling for any and everything in my life. Maybe it had something to do with growing up without a father or a positive male role model. I knew I longed to be loved in that way. As a young girl, I wanted to hear daddy's voice. Not to place blame because they were my choices, but I strongly believe that a father figure would have helped me to make better ones.

More pressures included me getting pregnant at age 14. After I told my child's father, he said that he was headed for college, only to find out years later that there was another girl pregnant.

The ending decision was having an abortion. Then, at age 15, during the summer, I was hanging out with some of my friends who I had grown up with in church. They became like sisters to me.

But on one summer evening while I was visiting them, I went with one of them to their boyfriend's family's house for a cookout and family gathering. Shortly after, we decided to go to her boyfriend's friend's apartment. There were these pictures of some pretty little girls. I told the friend how cute they were. We all sat down and laughed and began to talk. A little after that, I felt sick and lightheaded. I asked if I could use the restroom, and he showed me where it was. Now, I had remembered seeing a restroom somewhere else, but the one he took me to was inside of a bedroom. I closed the bathroom door, and I thought he had walked out of the bedroom.

While I was inside the restroom, I heard the music come on. At that moment, I was not thinking anything strange was going on. I just thought they decided to play music. What bothered me was how loud it was, and I was starting to get a headache. Once I finished inside the restroom, I opened the door and turned out the light, not really paying attention to anything. I turned the light out, looked up, and saw this guy sitting on the bed. As I tried to walk past him to open the bedroom door, he pulled my hand back and pushed me on the bed. Next thing

I knew, I was laying down, pants off, and this guy began to take advantage of me. I began to drift in and out as if I was conscious but unaware of what was going on around me. When he finished, I was still out of it, thinking to myself, what just happened? He opened the door and left. I came out shortly after that and just sat down by my friend. She looked at me and asked if I was okay. I don't remember leaving or getting into his car or him dropping us off. I just kept going in and out of being alert.

The next day was crazy. I really couldn't remember much. We went to church and then went to my friend's house. As we were getting out of the car, there was a man who pulled up next to the car, and he started speaking to my godfather. I looked at the man—he was the guy from the night before. He looked at me as if he had seen a ghost, and he left really quickly. I was scared so I just went into the house with everyone else.

Once summer was over, school started, and it was time for sports physicals. While waiting for my paperwork, the doctor came in and announced that I was unable to participate in track because I was pregnant. I couldn't tell my family what really took place over the summer. How would I explain that I was raped? Would they have believed me due to the past?

That night changed the rest of my life forever in so many

different ways, and one of those ways left me with a baby girl who I would raise. A baby girl who would never ever know her father because of that night. It opened up a door of hurt and pain that was unbearable. It opened up feelings of not being worthy, not loving myself, and a damaged heart that only God could fix, when I allowed Him to. I remained silent through the whispers, talks, and looks of people judging before they even knew the truth.

Although I was a mother, I had no idea what it meant and didn't learn until much later in life. As a young mother, I was still very much immature and still figuring things out. I did so many things wrong. I was very selfish, still with this hurt buried inside me. I married at a young age to the father of my daughter who had been child number four. The relationship did not last long at all. After that, my auntie past away; she had raised me and taught me everything I know. When I lost her, I could not bounce back at all. I was lost, and it took a long time to find my way back. I drank all the time to hide the pain. I was always working, and I left my oldest to fend for herself and her siblings.

**Pressure.**

My mother, whom I love very much, could only teach us what she learned from her mother. Sharing and talking about things was not a part of growing up, so the cycle repeated. She was able to teach us good work ethics that I appreciate dearly to this day. She also taught us how to have and value a relationship with God. I thank God for the people He placed in my life at different times to teach me—whether good or bad, it was all for the process.

**Pressure.**

For about 12 years, I allowed this guy to come in and out of my life when I wasn't married. I thought it was love. It was on my end, but to him I was just another test-drive dummy. This relationship got me two felonies, 73 days in jail, and years of tears, heartache, and disappointment in myself, on top of much embarrassment. The truth of the matter is, as much as I wanted to blame him, it was my choice. Stupidity! The other side to that is I had to realize if I had no love for myself, I needed to have some for my children. It took someone to tell me of the damage I was doing to the kids as well as myself to realize I needed to change. I had to love them enough to put a stop to it, but God took my bad choices and built character. He always works it out for our good. And it's important that we remember that He's the only one who can judge us. I am so happy that He is, and that He exams our lives the way no one could ever do. Unlike people, God weighs all evidence before coming to a final decision. God looks at everything, in every way. He sees what people do not see in you and/or will not see.

A diamond is judged by its color, clarity, carat, and cut. These are considered the Four Cs. The more you see the quality of the Four Cs, the more valuable the diamond becomes. God knows your brilliance, talent, and beauty, and He knows how to work out the heat and pressure we get ourselves into; He is just wonderful like that. Each process is created special, although we may have the same and/or similar stories. We endure differently, which makes our value increase. No two diamonds have ever had the same inclusion (meaning air bubbles, cracks, minerals, scratches, or chips), which makes each diamond unique and special.

People's opinions are based off of what they see, hear, or assume, but sometimes there's some truth too. However, if you don't know what you possess inside, you will start to believe the madness. As a diamond myself, I shared that some of my heat and pressures were rape, alcohol abuse, sex addiction, low self-esteem, no self-worth, and I can go on and on. You, on the other hand, may be able to share your pressures about drugs, prison, foster homes, etc. You get the picture.

There is only one you (hence the word "unique"). You can reach the people that no one else can. During the process, God takes us through trials which makes and shapes us. He uses heat and pressure to build us up again. He reconstructs all those wrong choices we've made, and then brings out what He has already put inside which is development, so that the light that we possess shines through.

Every obstacle, situation, and test is part of how a diamond is made. It's the roughness that God begins to cut away. It's the baggage He unpacks and the hurt He heals. It may hurt as He cuts on you, but you will never be the same afterwards. The cut defines you; the cutting process will show who you really are and what you were created to do. It also shows how special and valuable you are. Your defining moment is when you begin to realize that you have so much more to offer than what you have actually been giving out. You are the diamond that will shine at God's appointed time. Get ready as He prepares you for the next part of the process.

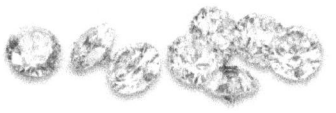

*What are the things that have damaged you?*

*What things can you start working on to heal?*

___
___
___
___
___
___
___
___
___
___
___
___

# Two

## THE DIAMOND CUTTING PROCESS

Diamond cutting is considered an art. It is done to change the form of the diamond, from a diamond rough to an actual diamond. This process changes the rock into the smooth stone that we know it to be.

A diamond cutter goes by the title of a gemologist and is required to have skill, knowledge, special tools, equipment, and various techniques in order to cut the rough stone. The cutter must know the exact location of all the flaws of the rough stone. On top of that, they have to make sure that the safety of the carat's weight is maintained in order for it to be valuable. The diamond cutter first observes the rough stone. Remember that in this state, the gem has no beauty, no luster, and you cannot see what the rough stone will become

The long lasting luster and its ability to transmit light are the particular beauties about the diamond. It also has the ability to bend. However, you will not see this take place until the third stage of the cutting process. This is the stage where the diamond is polished. The gemologist must keep three important rules in mind when they cut the rough stone. The first is to think about the cut itself, as it determines the true beauty of the diamond. The second rule to keep in mind is the weight of the diamond because it impacts the size of it. The last is removing flaws.

The diamond cutter examines the stone with a certain tool then decides how the stone should be shaped in order to keep the most weight and allow the most light to travel through. The cutter knows where every scratch, flaw, and streak are, and whether the imperfections are on the surface or deep in the heart of the stone. After that, the cutter goes to work. He uses a special wooden stick and ruler, which he fills with a sticky- or cement-like substance, as well as some clay mixed with sand. Using a lamp, he softens the cement, which is then fixed in the stone and around the diamond. Once it cools, the diamond is put in its place.

Now this is the special part. The gemologist then uses another diamond to cut a V-shape in the diamond rough. The V-shape must lay in the right direction of the stone. This task calls for the cutter to be highly trained and skilled. The cutter uses a box and a little sifter to catch the dust once the diamond powder drops. When the V-shape is cut deep enough, the cutter holds the wooden stick and ruler in one hand and he hits the ruler with the other hand to break the stone.

The slightest mistake can forever damage the diamond's value. Yet, the task is done with ease and without hesitation; this process is called lapidary which means it will be long and complicated. The stone must be cut in a way that gives the diamond the most value. Most diamonds are shaped like an octahedron, which is an eight-sided flat surface. Two stones can be made out of the octahedron with little weight loss of the diamond. If they are not formed normally, or cannot form at all, the imperfections will be present in the wrong place.

The cut of the diamond is considered because it affects how much light the diamond will reflect. The balance, dimensions, and shape are also considered. You will know that a diamond is well cut if it reflects a great quality of light. Likewise, poorly cut diamonds do not reflect well. Types of cuts include ideal cuts, which are fair, good, very good, and excellent cuts. Examples like fancy cuts are oval or shaped like a pear.

Marcel Tolkowsky is a highly renowned gemologist, known to be the father of the round brilliant cut diamonds. Tolkowsky learned that if a diamond was cut deep then it would cause the light to disperse out of both sides of the diamond. Basically, this means that the stone would lose the light, fire and sparkle it possessed. Tolkowsky's idea was that in order to receive the best appearance inside and outside of the diamond, it had to reflect light from different locations. Therefore, he created the ideal cut on the diamond. Other cuts include:

*Rose Cuts:*

Antique gems used to repair or make a duplicate copy.

*Step Cuts:*

Makes the diamond's beauty, clarity, and whiteness show.

*Passion Cuts:*

Gives the diamond a greater light, or beauty to the diamond.

*Princess Cuts:*

Brings an awareness to the diamond's beauty and shine rather than just light.

*Double Cuts:*

Shows its shine when the fire is increased.


There are different cuts to form a diamond, all for one purpose which is to bring the most out of that particular gem. Think of God as the cutter and in order for you to get to your brilliant light and the beauty that's inside you, God must send you through the cutting process which seems very hard, long, and complicated. God is so amazing. Just as the cutter has a responsibility to keep the diamond protected and to maintain its safety, God does too as the gemologist of His gems, His people.

Everything is not good for you, so He has to take those things away. He will also replace what He took and pour into you what He knows will take you to the next level of value. For instance, God cuts away hurt, pain, hatred, anger, etc. People who are not here for your growth and development, but only want to be a burden. God will replace those negative things with people who encourage you with love, peace, joy, patience, happiness, wisdom, understanding, and so much more.

God had to do some major cutting in me. To name a few that I know had to be cut: cheating, lying, stealing, being promiscuous, and grieving the loss of loved ones. That's not even half, but I am so grateful He did. At the time, I had no idea God was using those things that He cut away to teach and discipline me into a place where I would never want to do those things again. And because of how awesome He is, He replaced them with strength, peace, love, and an intimate relationship with Him—just as He did Paul in 2 Corinthians. God cuts every rough edge and smooths every rough surface.

God removed everything that could become a hindrance to my growth and value, but at the same time allowed things to happen for the same reason. For every bad situation, I have learned to get closer to God more and more, as well as the good ones. You must be close to Him because people can be for you one minute and against you the next. And you will need Him to lean on. Your focus has to be totally on God. Remember, it is the fire and pressure that forms a diamond, so it's pressure and fire that you will have to embrace in order to receive your full value. God gave me an ideal cut. It's a not-so-perfect gem and to get the best out of me, He had to reflect His light from many different angles to get a smooth gem. As a matter of fact, He did more than one.

God knows the balance of light and fire to use; He knows just how much we can take, even if we do not think we are strong enough ourselves. God does certain cuts on different gems, but it is all for one purpose and that is to get you to where you can reflect the light and beauty that you possess.

One cut repairs and reproduces other pieces, meaning you can help restore and encourage someone by having clarity of God's word. You can give revelation and insight to scriptures reflecting His beauty and light. You may see this in our pastors or elders. Others are designed to make a person greater in value by showing them self-worth or helping them with self-esteem and celebrating one another. This can be done by just acknowledging how beautiful or talented they are. The cutting process is long and complicated because God gets rid of our flaws, pain, and trust issues. Just imagine: He has to go behind every bad choice, switch it around for your good, and when He's finished with your past, it becomes a motivational tool. He gets rid of all those unnecessary things, so He can get the maximum beauty and value out of us, while being careful of the cut—not to damage or destroy, but to handle us with care. And He does these things all while keeping us safe.

You may be small in the eyes of man, but you were created to affect lives. In God's eyes, you are a giant and others know you are as well. It is sad when we do not even know that about ourselves. Don't allow your view to become tainted by what other people think or say about you. You are so much more than that. You are more than your past, brighter than your future, and more amazing than your present situations. You are that bright light in a room full of darkness. Your presence alone makes their days exciting, whether they want to admit it or not.

You have it going on with your gifted and anointed self. People really are afraid of you. People really want what you have. It is crazy that we take it for granted because we think so negatively about ourselves that we cannot even see what we have on the inside. The gemologist takes his time and makes sure he is calm and in control. That says a lot about God's love for us. No matter how difficult we are, He remains collected so He can cut us perfectly with no splitting or imperfections.

Forget people! Forget the past! Forget the mistakes! Forget the lies! Forget the truth of who you once were. Stay focused on what is front of you…a *brilliant* better you!

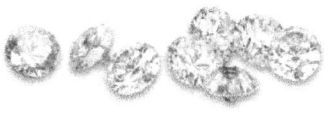

*What change would you like to see happen in your life?*

*How can you begin to change those things you see?*

# Three

## PLANNING STAGE

This is a simple but serious process that examines the stone closely from a value point of view. There are two decisions that are made about the cut of the stone: Will the greatest value for the stone be received, and how soon can the diamond be sold once it is finished. God's process of planning is to see how you can be shaped, made, and molded for His use. You are a hand-picked rough stone. God looks and says, (Your name) has been through alcohol abuse, rape, emotional abuse, sickness, and pain. Now how can I use these things for better? God begins to plan and start the process of changing, replacing, adding this, and taking away that, meanwhile showing grace, mercy and unconditional love. He gives ideas, changes your mindset, and equips you with all the tools to reach your full potential. Your potential is more than just having a title. Titles are not everything, although God has created pastors, teachers, doctors, etc. Do not allow titles to make you feel inadequate.

They are just titles. It is okay to be ordinary and have the same power to affect someone's life. It is your beauty being revealed. It's the endless tasks. It could be a smile, an embrace, a kind gesture, or even a sweet word that alone could stop a person from committing suicide, overcome depression, and not feel as lonely.

For example, when a person stared at me, being the diamond in the rough, I would reply with a disgusted look or respond in a negative manner. You know how we do, or just give them the meanest face we have. You cannot help but to laugh, and not only is it not funny, but it is so immature and childish. But that was just insecurity talking, a lack of acceptance, and having no self-worth. I know you have heard the old saying of hurt people hurt people. There might not be anything wrong with the person, but we see our own defeat and try to push that fear off onto the other person. Once we are healed and made whole from our own brokenness, we don't damage anyone else because we have the confidence we need to succeed. When God changes our mindset, His beauty reflects light and brings notice to you. Therefore, it becomes a habit to smile and say a kind word and just know that someone is only admiring God's beauty inside you. It is okay to smile or give a compliment. It will take nothing away from you. In fact, it enhances just how beautiful you really are.

Now God can begin to use you for His glory. He intends on doing something wonderful with you and for you, if you allow Him to. It is all a part of His perfect plan that He has for your life. I am only sharing with you what I know *personally*. God plans to do some awesome work with you and through you. It will not be easy. However, if you allow Him to do what He does best, the process will be much easier.

*Even though I've been damaged.*
*God has shown me that I am still valuable.*
*You were ready to throw me away, because I didn't seem to be beautiful.*
*You weren't able to see the light that was hidden within.*
*You wanted to discard me. Ignore me.*
*But what if you took a minute to see. I mean really look inside.*
*You would see the beauty. You would see the light.*
*But yet you walk over me like I don't matter,*
*Even though it hurts my very soul. You think I am just a lump of coal.*
*I know that you can't see what God sees.*
*If you could, I would not be treated so poorly.*
*Thrown away and left for destruction.*
*When all you had to do was uncover the blackness that covered my soul.*
*Meaning that you took time to show me, teach me, and love me.*
*But instead you laughed and judged me.*

*But God came along and He took his time to shape, make, and mold me.*

*If beauty is in the eye of the beholder. I am so glad He was the one to take over.*

*He showed me who I am. He fixed me and changed my very soul. He found what you could not. He saw me beyond the tears, sadness, and pain.*

*He cut away all the things that had me trapped and made me into the diamond that I am to be.*

*I am not damaged. I am valuable. And this light He placed inside me will never go away.*

*I am A Diamond In the Rough!*

– Shaloria Mitchell

# EXERCISE

I want you to take a selfie.

Begin to look at it and see how wonderful you are. Begin to change the way you think of yourself and remind yourself daily how unique and special you are.

Post your selfie on Facebook and Instagram with this hashtag: #Diamondsthatshine

*How can the rough situations in your life be used for better?*

_____

_____

_____

_____

_____

_____

_____

_____

_____

_____

_____

# *Four*

## MAXIMIZING VALUE

The diamond's utility is measured by the greatest value. This process is in choosing a strategy that will benefit the seller of the diamond. Some have it down to a science; it is definitely an art for a stone to go from its roughness into a polished gem. The choice of the cut is done by the shape, the imperfections that need to be removed, and its weight. The first step into finding out how soon the diamond will be finished is to determine how much a person is willing to pay. The second is determining how soon the diamond can sell, how it is cut, how the light is reflected, and the fire and pressure it will go through. Because the diamond rough is cut at an angle, its thickness, depth, and smoothness is questioned. The light has to shine through it. The slightest mistake in the size or angle will affect its light and therefore its value.

God knows when and how to prepare you. He knows how and when to cut you: what you can take and when you can take it, what to put in the fire, how hot to make the fire, and exactly how much pressure you can stand. Even when we don't think we can handle it, God knows we can. We are important and have to stop thinking down about ourselves. God knows our worth. He already knows He will receive a return on His investment.

At times, I've felt worthless and that I did not deserve the best. I thought I was nothing and often settled for less. But when I looked in the mirror and saw myself like God saw me—as a tool being refined—I began to find the love for myself and the love God had for me. With all my flaws, mistakes, failures, heartaches, disappointments, and confusions, God was willing to look past that and make me into the diamond I was destined to be: a light to those who felt the same but needed a voice. God increased my value so I could be marketable, meaning I could relate to issues, circumstances, and similar situations to those wanting change and not knowing how to overcome or why they are going through what they are going through.

I think to myself, would it have been different if my father were around, acknowledged me, wrote a letter or two, and even called? Just to say to me that he knows me, and he is thinking about me. Even if he said he couldn't be there for whatever reason would have been cool with me. It was the silence that hurt the most. Maybe it wouldn't have made a difference, but at least the effort would have been made.

The crazy thing is that I saw this guy on Facebook, and he looked so much like this picture that I had of my father, so I reached out to him and inboxed him. I asked him if his father's name was my dad's name because he looked young in his picture, and on his profile, his name was James instead of Jimmy. I asked him if his dad ever went by Jimmy. He replied, "No, but I have," so I checked his birth date and saw he would have been the same age as my father. I asked him if he knew my mother. I gave him her name and the city and state where he would have met her. After that, he blocked me. So to me, that was him saying, yes, I am your father, but I am not ready to acknowledge you yet. The feelings of rejection from not having him around created a low self-esteem that I shouldn't have had to deal with otherwise. But regardless of if he is or will ever be in my life, I still have to fight for me. Either I will let this define who I am or I will define me.

Life and death lies in the power of the tongue, so be careful what comes out of your mouth. Your words have power. No more negative talking. No more saying what you don't have. No more saying who you are not. Start speaking positive. Look at yourself in the mirror and speak life: I am beautiful, talented and worth it! I have plenty of things to offer. I am great! I am a beautiful creation of God. I am mighty and strong! In the famous words of Beyonce, "You Slay, I Slay, We Slay, All Day… OK!" I am a diamond and can manifest anything that I put my mind to.

*"I can do all things through Christ who strengthens me."*
– Philippians 4:13

# EXERCISE

Write down some of your favorite things about yourself. Begin to say them out loud while facing the mirror. A good time to say these things would be when you wake up in the morning or are getting ready for bed.

For example, some positive thoughts would be:

I am beautiful.

I love me.

I am proud of myself.

I love my eyes.

I can make it.

*Start with I...*

# Five

## WEIGHT RETENTION

The weight of the diamond affects the appearance in the diamond's value and size. The price of the diamond increases when the weight increases. The most popular cut is also considered. The weight will show if the stone is the best of the finished stones as it relates to the carat. A diamond has more weight before it is cut because it has extra around it. However, it does not improve the beauty; it just has added weight. How much weight do you think you hold?

You have great influence in others' lives. You hold so much importance. Everything you've seen, everything you've been through…people either know or think they know. Your life has been an open book to some people, and people are watching whether you notice it or not. You have not given up and that is inspiring to many. Those closest to you have not given up all because of little ole you. You help them keep moving. You hold a particular position in someone's life—voluntarily or not.

We go through so much as young ladies and women. It seems as if no one really understands the things we do for our families and friends. No one can imagine the face we put on in order to hide the things we feel. If we know how we feel, then we should know how another young lady feels. But instead, we treat each other like we can't relate, or we don't know what heartache feels like—hurt, disappointment, and rejection. We don't know how to become sympathetic or show empathy for our fellow sister. We are so quick to pass judgment and assume things about the young lady without knowing her walk, her story. We forget to live in the moment and celebrate each other.

It's as if our love is conditional, and it is conditional because the majority of us don't know how to love because we never saw what love is; therefore, we don't even love ourselves. But what happens when you learn to love yourself? What happens when you see yourself the way God sees you, and loves you? We know God loves us unconditionally. WE know that He gave up His only son for us. Now if this is not love, can you imagine your favorite person in the whole world dying for not only you but your haters? You have so much influence—the way you walk, talk, or carry yourself. You have the influence to carry love, show love, give love, and feel love. You walk in the room and all eyes are on you. You either can take it, leave, or you can smile and empower some other young lady or woman to be as confident as you are. You have to be careful of the weight you hold. You can either damage a flower or you can help it grow. You have the juice now—what will you do with it?

The weight you carry is amazing! Your value is more than you can imagine. You have the ability to produce life-changing shifts in others' lives. Your weight retention as a diamond causes others to let their light shine, helping them to reach their full potential. Your life experiences and how you handle different situations allows you to sway and affect people. Sometimes God places you in a person's life at a divine appointed time on a job, in a store, on the playground, etc. You never know just how much you mean to a person or how much influence you may have on someone.

Weight retention also means gaining something. What are you gaining? Is it power, love, respect, strength, courage, or wisdom? God will empower you with whatever is needed. You may think you are nothing, but you are huge in God's eyes and you will need all that your testimony entails to be a major factor in someone's life.

*"If I give everything I own to the poor and even go to the stake to be burned as a martyr, but I don't love, I've gotten nowhere. So, no matter what I say, what I believe, and what I do, I'm bankrupt without love."* – Corinthians 13:4-7 (MSG)

*Love never gives up.*
*Love cares more for others than for self.*
*Love doesn't want what it doesn't have.*
*Love doesn't strut,*
*Doesn't have a swelled head,*
*Doesn't force itself on others,*
*Isn't always "me first,"*
*Doesn't fly off the handle,*
*Doesn't keep score of the sins of others,*
*Doesn't revel when others grovel,*
*Takes pleasure in the flowering of truth,*
*Puts up with anything,*
*Trusts God always,*
*Always looks for the best,*
*Never looks back,*
*But keeps going to the end.*

—1 Corinthians 13

You can be beat to capacity with Mac lips and all and still be rude, nasty, and messy inside; and what is inside eventually comes out, so all the make-up in the world could never cover up the lack of love we have for each other.

I AM MY SISTER'S KEEPER.

## EXERCISE

Call your BFF (someone that doesn't mind telling you the truth) and ask her in what ways do you influence her.

Ask what makes her want to be your friend.

Now if she says positive things, ask how you can show that to everyone else.

If it is negative, you know it is time for a look in the mirror again. It's time to change the negative things that you see.

*What negative things do you need to change?*

_____

_____

_____

_____

_____

_____

_____

_____

_____

_____

_____

# Six

## COLOR RETENTION

The way that the light reflects through the diamond produces different sensations to the eye. A cut can make the color of the diamond. This causes the diamond to have a higher value. Some cuts are used to bring more of the color out of the diamond by sending light or heat that creates a glowing bright light. As a diamond clears, the more valuable it is, ranging from D (colorless) to Z (heavily tinted). A diamond with no color allows the light to pass through easier; it allows the light to be seen as a rainbow. It takes years of experience and a trained eye to grade diamonds.

2 Timothy 3:17 notes "that the man of God may be complete, thoroughly equipped for every good work." This is the process in which we lose our own identity, where we start living for Christ and stop doing our own thing. No matter what is said or done, we begin to put God's business first and become more

Christ-like. As Ephesians 6: 13 points out, you should "therefore take up the whole armor of God. That you may be able to withstand in the evil day, and having done all, to stand." Put on the armor of God. No need to be afraid as you lose yourself and gain the things of God. The more colorless you become, the more valuable you are. Pride or selfishness is done and God gives humbleness and love. Begin to see people the way God sees people. We often forget where we come from and what it took to get us here. We have the nerve to look down on and talk about others in their cutting process, as if we were never cut and have never been through similar situations or worse. Who are we to judge? No one has it completely together. What happened to encouraging words designed to help push people in the right direction? For this is how we become colorless. We are treasures to God. Our value is priceless because the maximum return on God's investment is far more than money. You help save lives. It should be less of you and more of God at this point. It is not about us, but all about God.

Matthew 5:1-16

*1-2 When Jesus saw his ministry drawing huge crowds, he climbed a hillside. Those who were apprenticed to him, the committed, climbed with him. Arriving at a quiet place, he sat down and taught his climbing companions. This is what he said:*

*³ "You're blessed when you're at the end of your rope. With less of you there is more of God and his rule.*

*⁴ "You're blessed when you feel you've lost what is most dear to you. Only then can you be embraced by the One most dear to you.*

*⁵ "You're blessed when you're content with just who you are—no more, no less. That's the moment you find yourselves proud owners of everything that can't be bought.*

*⁶ "You're blessed when you've worked up a good appetite for God. He's food and drink in the best meal you'll ever eat.*

*⁷ "You're blessed when you care. At the moment of being 'care-full,' you find yourselves cared for.*

*⁸ "You're blessed when you get your inside world—your mind and heart—put right. Then you can see God in the outside world.*

*⁹ "You're blessed when you can show people how to cooperate instead of compete or fight. That's when you discover who you really are, and your place in God's family.*

*¹⁰ "You're blessed when your commitment to God provokes persecution. The persecution drives you even deeper into God's kingdom.*

*11-12* "Not only that—count yourselves blessed every time people put you down or throw you out or speak lies about you to discredit me. What it means is that the truth is too close for comfort and they are uncomfortable. You can be glad when that happens—give a cheer, even! —for though they don't like it, I do! And all heaven applauds. And know that you are in good company. My prophets and witnesses have always gotten into this kind of trouble.

*13* "Let me tell you why you are here. You're here to be salt-seasoning that brings out the God-flavors of this earth. If you lose your saltiness, how will people taste godliness? You've lost your usefulness and will end up in the garbage.

*14-16* "Here's another way to put it: You're here to be light, bringing out the God-colors in the world. God is not a secret to be kept. We're going public with this, as public as a city on a hill. If I make you light-bearers, you don't think I'm going to hide you under a bucket, do you? I'm putting you on a light stand. Now that I've put you there on a hilltop, on a light stand—shine! Keep open house; be generous with your lives. By opening up to others, you'll prompt people to open up with God, this generous Father in heaven."

Matthew 5:1-16 shows us how to take on an attitude of Jesus. Once we adopt a state of bliss, it becomes easier for us to treat people how we want to be treated; even if they don't, we still can. God is telling us how blessed we are when we take on these attitudes. Verse 11 goes further and says "blessed are you when people insult you, persecute you and falsely say all kinds of evil against you because of me." Verse 12 tells us to "rejoice and be glad because great is your reward in heaven, for in the same way they persecuted the prophets who were before you."

We are in a win-win situation. We are good both ways and even more blessed when colorless. God is with us while we are doing His work now *and* we will have a great reward in heaven.

*"And let us not grow weary while doing good, for in due season we shall reap if we do not lose heart."* –Galatians 6:9

This chapter says a lot about how you can get ready and prepared to handle people and do your best to become a better you. It talks about the things that you may need in order to transform into greater. All these scriptures are saying is that here are some tools that can help you. If you read them and apply them, you will come out on top. Some things are better said than done. It might take you a while to get to the point of changing things about yourself that have been held deep inside. Most things we have are defense shields and walls of protection to keep your heart safe. But there comes a time when we have to look into our pain, learn from it, let it be used to push us forward, and not allow it to hold us from experiencing great things, whether good or bad. WE have to learn to shake those off and push that reset button, which allows us to start over again.

*What are the things in your life that are stopping you from being great?*

___
___
___
___
___
___
___
___
___
___

# Seven

## MAXIMIZATION TURNAROUND STAGE

This is the stage where it is determined how quickly the diamond will sell. While the cut can determine how soon it will sell, it also must show a continual promise of attaining more buyers for diamonds. This is the stage where God sees how soon you are going to do His work. This is where God turns your life around and puts you back on track. How quickly you are going to act on what He called you to do? The sooner you get it together, the sooner you will help others. The quicker you allow God to cleanse you and put you to work, the faster His investment returns unto Him.

When it comes to God preparing you for His work, He makes no mistakes. Whatever He feels like leaving behind to help you, He will. You should start to know your purpose. What makes you happy? What do you enjoy doing and adding to ministry? Prepare yourself with God's word and anything you feel will enhance your knowledge of who He really is.

God is ready for you to carry out His work by using everything He has equipped you with. Most of us say we can tell when someone is lying or when someone is fake. Those are gifts from God—gifts of discernment, wisdom, encouragement, and so on. What makes you special and unique? Use it and do it unto God's glory while embracing others. Keep moving forward, and whatever God has put into you will come out. His word does not return unto Him void, meaning it will not come back with no effect or force. But rather that it will be complete and set out to do what it was created to do.

How much are you worth? Are you replaceable? How do you help the people around you? You matter! The things you do matter. The things you say matter. You may not be able to please everyone, but what you have inside of you is a wonderful gift to share with your friends, family, another lady, and even the world. Now it is your time to know what that is and make your day better.

*"So shall My word be that goes forth from My mouth; It shall not return to Me void, But it shall accomplish what I please, And it shall prosper in the thing for which I sent it."* –Isaiah 55:11

*What are your gifts and talents?*

_____

_____

_____

_____

_____

_____

_____

_____

_____

_____

_____

*What are the things that make up who you are?*

*How can you use those things to help another person?*

*Who will you help?*

*How will you use them to help yourself?*

_____

_____

_____

_____

_____

_____

_____

_____

_____

_____

_____

# Eight

## CLEAVING STAGE

Cleaving means to cut, divide, split, or separate. In this stage, the rough stone is divided into separate pieces so each piece can be finished as different diamonds. And the rough stone is cut into a nice size. Cleaving is important when it comes to large and valuable stones because you can get different sizes. However, not all diamonds need to be divided. Some diamonds are found in good condition. If you try to divide the diamond the wrong way, you can shatter it. If a diamond rough is surrounded with cement, then the V-shape is cut into it using another diamond as a means to cut it. The condition of the diamond and its ability for it to separate depends on its strength.

Sometimes it is necessary for God to separate you from people. Oftentimes, we may feel as if we are rejected, but really it is God's way of telling us we need a little tender, love, and care from God. He needs us to fully focus on Him, so He leads us into the right direction by turning us away from everything that is not like Him. At this point, we are sound in mind, knowing how to hear God and allow His Holy Spirit to be our eyes.

It is not important at all for everyone to like you because everybody will not, no matter how much love you show and no matter how nice you are. People serve a purpose in your life; some come to encourage you and some come to discourage you or throw you off your game with distractions. Some will be there forever, and some will be there for just a little while, but whatever the case may be, whether it's expected or unexpected, it is not your concern to find the why or how. That will only drive you insane. But allow it to become positive motivation, set goals, and move forward.

Even though some things may be hurtful, like losing a best friend, a loved one, or anyone you thought would be around for the long run. You must know that things will only get better. I think the worst thing for me were unexpected deaths in my family—people who I love with all of me. My sister was one of them. The pain that I felt from that, it was not in my nature to grab ahold of why. But as I dealt with the pain of losing my best friend, I knew it moved something inside of me that made me want to do something and make a difference somehow and in some way. I looked at the things she went through. I wanted to make it my business that another young lady or woman would not have to go through the same struggle of loving themselves and wanting better for their lives. Know how beautiful you are and do not settle for less, but actually have what you deserve, which is love and the best that His life has to offer.

I wonder every day, if things had been different. Did she know her worth? That burns inside of me, and this is the message that I need to tell every young lady and every woman—just how amazing, wonderful, and awesome you are. And although I can't bring my sister back, she will always live in my heart. I had to realize that maybe, just maybe, this had to happen to light a fire under me. So I will not just think about it, but I will actually go to work and do something about it. I have to, and you have to go beyond what you feel and see that no matter what, you must never allow anyone or anything to ruin or dull the shine and light within you. You may not know what the reason is, but what if the reason is you? Someone is waiting on you, and everything that may need to go away or leave you is not to make you hurt, but to actually shine a light on what you have, and just maybe, it happens to bring that light inside out for all to see.

Distractions may turn our focus to things that God feels we don't need to engage in. Therefore, He separates us from these things. Separation is not so bad and it will be for the greater good in the long run. It's a process of isolation. At times, God wants you to Himself. Other times, He'll have you around people. Allow the separation to take place. It is for your growth and development, and it also helps to depend on God for everything during your time of separation.

Prayer and having an intimate relationship with God is the key. This is not for those who know this. It is for those who are overlooked and looked down on. People don't even realize you are the one who holds their blessing in your mouth. When we learn to uplift one another, and not assume the worst about each other, we can be very powerful together. I enjoyed my separation process. God gave me a *huge* look at me, myself, and I. As I allowed God to change and give direction, it allowed good to flow in me like never before. I wouldn't change this walk for anything.

Although many were wondering what I may have been doing and why I was away from church, I didn't care. All I knew was that God poured into me like never before, and I was finally ready for Him to release it in my life. Though it is an everyday process, I thank God that I am nothing like what I used to be. After my separation, I went back to church, changed for the better, and made room for God to release me and make a return on His investment.

*What may be some things that you need to get rid of in your life?*

*Who are the people who should be cut off?*

*Where are the places you should stop going?*

*What are the things you should stop doing?*

# Nine

## BRUTING STAGE

Bruting is a process where great physical force is used, where the grinding of the two diamonds take place. The diamonds are set in a spinning axle turning in opposite directions. They grind together in order to form a round shape. And the process is used as another way a rough stone is shaped. "As iron sharpens iron, so a man sharpens the countenance of his friend (Proverbs 27:17). We often want our secret to be kept quiet; sometimes it's failure and other times it is success. We are either ashamed or prideful, not knowing the impact we have or will have. As I said in the beginning, we never know how our life will make a difference.

For example, in dealing with death, I found comfort in a bottle. So much so that I could not get to the point of intoxication anymore. The same went for sex, where I often experimented. Just think how important it would have been if I had one person say, "I know death can be unimaginable, but if you just cry it out and take one day at a time, it'll help to ease the pain." Or just some encouraging words, or maybe even a hug.

I don't think liquor and sex would have had a chance to take over if someone had told me curiosity really does kill the cat. I didn't know I opened a door for such a strong spirit. It took much prayer and fasting to get rid of that spirit. I wish I had someone to warn me about that one for sure. I would have never been that curious ever, but the good thing about that was I was able to warn someone else of what lay ahead of that road and they did not walk down it.

I tried filling a void with many things, but nothing came close to taking the pain away. These things need to be dealt with in order for you not to make mistakes based off of hurt. Sometimes emotions are attached to what was done to you. As I mentioned before, hurt people hurt people. You might ask, how can I love or trust and even be a good friend if I don't know how to be? If it was never demonstrated to me? This is when you have to decide to let go of all the hurt and pain that's holding you back to become a better you. If you want to move forward, forgiveness and healing must take place.

*Amen!* And the list goes on and on. If I can watch out for my fellow brothers and sisters and encourage them to keep moving, let them know they are not alone, then I will. By being a witness, do you know how much harm or danger we can save others from? Everything you encounter can help someone else either overcome what they're going through or warn them not to do the same. You're a diamond sharpening another diamond for greatness.

Anything I've been through, I'm willing to share—not for attention, but just wanting you to know that you are not by yourself. We are in this together. We should never be too high and mighty that we forget where we come from, or even assume someone is not where we are. Never think less of someone simply because they don't do what you do or do it the way that you do. It is okay to be different. If everyone was the same, wouldn't the world be boring? I have watched people turn their nose up or look down on me because they figured I did not have a relationship with God. I was just different and different is good.

*"The wound is the place where the light enters you"* –Rumi

*What have you been through?*

*How can you use your story to help a friend?*

*How can you focus on forgiving and healing from hurt so you won't hurt others?*

# *Ten*

## POLISHING PROCESS

This process is to make the diamond shine or to refine it. In this stage, the diamond is improved by the removing all its impurities. This is the final stage of the cutting process. In the polish process, the first step is called blocking. Blocking can polish up to eighteen diamonds at one time on a polishing disc with an electric motor. It is charged with the diamond powder that was collected by the cutter at the first stage. Here is where we shine like new money. Here is where it all becomes worth it. Here is where we say we would do it all over again. If we knew it would end this way, life couldn't be better now. After all, we made it. Finally, we know why. Well, at least that's what I tell myself these days.

It is amazing to see where God has brought me. I may not be there all the way, but one thing is for certain: I am nothing like I was. After God has broken us down and has rebuilt us, we are ready for what He has in store. He has taken us from the dirt and removed all filthiness. Now we are being polished to shine just the way diamonds were meant to shine.

Diamonds are beautiful. However, dust and dirt can make them lose their sparkle. When diamonds become dull in appearance, it damages their value. By keeping them polished on a regular basis not only will you protect the beauty, but you will ensure its worth and condition. There are jewelry cleaners you can purchase, and even better, you can take the diamond to a jeweler and have it polished. Doing these simple things will ensure the maintenance of the value forever. As you know, you are the true diamond. Here are a few tips to ensure your maintenance:

- ◊ Learn about God. Find an incredible place to go for worship.
- ◊ Look for a mentor.
- ◊ Find things that interest you to become better and want better (books, classes, etc.)
- ◊ Surround yourself with supporters and positive people.
- ◊ Motivate and encourage yourself.
- ◊ Keep out all negativity (even your own negative thoughts).

You may get one or two in the bunch who are not who they portrayed themselves to be, but don't let them damage your shine. It is okay to live life and enjoy it. Just because we are doing God's work doesn't mean we have to be dull and boring. He not only wants you to live, but to live life to the fullest—to be well-supplied with everything you may need *and want*. When you understand God's unconditional love, you want to be obedient just to make Him smile. And when you happen to slip and make a mistake, because you will, get the cleaner out, wipe yourself off, and continue to shine. God's word is truly amazing, and what He reveals in it will be a help of a lifetime.

I used to think reading the Bible was hard to get into and boring, but I quickly found out that it was exciting. And once I got into it, I could not put it down. Using a dictionary or a concordance helps as well. Then you can start meditating on a verse to help you get through your day. The more you read, the more it enhances the brightness, and the more you enhance your brightness, the more your beauty is revealed and the more valuable you become. Don't be afraid to shine your light!

*"When you see a good person, think of becoming like him/her. When you see someone not so good, reflect on your own weak points."* – Confucius

*Make a list of things you can do to improve your sparkle.*

___
___
___
___
___
___
___
___
___
___
___
___

## *Eleven*

## THE FINAL INSPECTION

The final inspection is the last stage. The diamond is examined carefully, closely, and critically. The diamonds are cleaned and inspected for the last time for any flaws. During this step, the diamonds are cleaned in acids, so that there will be no flaws, spots, or blemishes.

Who wants a diamond with a crack in it? Who wants to pay all that money on a diamond that doesn't shine and sparkle? Who wants a diamond that has not been through the right amount of pressure and the right amount of heat to produce the best quality of a gem ever imaginable? No one wants a fake diamond! Many people can't afford the quality of a real diamond so they settle for cubic zirconia. But the downfall with cubic zirconia is that it doesn't last. Its endurance and quality is forced because it is man-made. The temperature and heat are applied at a rapid speed to hurry along the process of being made. But we know that diamonds last forever, and they have a beauty and shine that cannot be duplicated by the fakes. Go through the process, even when the heat and pressure feels unbearable, even when you feel like you want to get up, when you think you are not worth it because of low self-esteem and not loving yourself. Going through the process will change you in ways that will only make you greater.

At this stage, God is asking how ready you are. If you have to go back to the cutting board, then so be it. That just means God has found something that may hinder you in the long run and He wants to take care of that now before you go to work. I had to go back several times to get cut on. It took me years to learn how to sustain from having sex. I slipped up many of times, but due to God's grace and mercy—and an eventual made up mind—I was able to. Building a relationship with God gave me everything I needed.

God started removing people who didn't belong in my path and started placing the ones that He wanted there. We begin to help each other out spiritually, always motivating each other to continue down the path God has set before us. Even if you have lost clarity for a while, it is time to get back in the fire. Finish the work He started in you. We are supposed to be helpers to one another.

I would be less of a woman, sister, friend, and child of God to see anyone go through what I've been through and not step in. I cannot sit back and watch as someone else is struggling and frustrated while I have the keys to help push them and share with them what I've done to overcome. We all have keys to motivate, inspire, encourage, and to be a blessing to someone else, regardless of who it is and what it may be.

You will never be alone. Someone, somewhere has gone through what you have and made it. However, their process may not look like yours. What it took for them may not be the same for you. I would have been good with just a warning; I didn't need to learn the hard way. We can walk this out together, but that's where we fail with each other. No one wants to walk it out with us, but don't worry because God is there to walk, run, and even carry us if we need Him to.

If I see anyone—friends, family, strangers, even the haters—taking a rest from this race, I'm going to offer water, a headband, a towel, another pair of shoes, a massage, or run alongside of them for a couple of miles. I will always offer help, especially to my beautiful haters. Why can't we do that? When we begin to think and act Christ-like, we have passed inspection. It is no longer about us, but about God and what He would have us to do, even when we may not want to. Going into final inspection, your mindset will be that you would love to do it regardless of how you are feeling.

Then we become our most valuable, beautifully created selves. From a rough gem to a wonderful cut stone, better known as a diamond. You are unbreakable, able to withstand tough circumstances. You are unable to be destroyed and will not crack under pressure. In fact, pressure and heat makes you most beautiful and most valuable. Now let your light shine!

*Let your light so shine before men, that they may see your good works and glorify your Father in heaven.* –Matthew 5:16

*What is blocking you from your shine?*

_____

_____

_____

_____

_____

_____

_____

_____

_____

_____

_____

*What are the things you need to get rid of to pass inspection?*

# *Twelve*

## THE CARAT, CUT, COLOR, AND CLARITY OF A DIAMOND

Now that the final inspection is done, these are four characteristics that the experts use in helping consumers make the right decision for purchasing a diamond:

- ◊ The carat: how much influence you have
- ◊ The cut: how valuable are you to God
- ◊ The color: letting your light shine bright
- ◊ The clarity: becoming flawless

Sometimes it seems like we walk this journey by ourselves, but truly we are not alone. As I have mentioned before, we must be helpers to one another. We have to talk about and share those secrets, flaws, disappointments, and even successes, so we can motivate each other to keep running and not give up. It never said the race was given to the swift or to the strong. It stated that it was given to one who endured to the end.

You may fall, but don't stay down. Get back up! You may have to bandage yourself up for whatever injury you incur, but you get up and keep it moving. Don't look back and don't allow others to make you look back. Don't keep dwelling on the past, especially that which you cannot change. It's done, it's over. Stay focused by keeping your eyes on what's in front of you. You have everything you need, and what you don't have, God will show you how to obtain. You had to go through it all. It was all a part of your process to make you a beautifully created DIAMOND!

*For I know the thoughts that I think toward you, saith the LORD, thoughts of peace, and not of evil, to give you an expected end.*
–Jeremiah 29:11

# Reflections

# Notes

# About the Author

**Shaloria Michaela Mitchell** is a bestselling author and founder of Beautifully Created LLC, an organization that develops mentoring programs dedicated to motivating young ladies and women to increase their value by promoting their self-esteem and self-worth.

Shaloria is committed to helping women unlock their potential and activate their purpose. Having completed her associate's in human services, she is currently pursuing her bachelor's degree in psychology. Shaloria enjoys creative writing, as well as participating in empowerment workshops and seminars. In fact, she is also a motivational speaker teaching on topics such as self-discovery, self-love, and confidence.

Shaloria currently resides in Grand Rapids, Michigan, with

her four amazing children who are reflections of the certifying creed that she lives by:

*"Thank you for making me so wonderfully complex! Your workmanship is marvelous—how well I know it."*
–Psalm 139:14

    Stay in contact with Shaloria by visiting:
    **www.about.me/Shaloria.com**

## CREATING DISTINCTIVE BOOKS WITH INTENTIONAL RESULTS

We're a collaborative group of creative masterminds with a mission to produce high-quality books to position you for monumental success in the marketplace.

Our professional team of writers, editors, designers, and marketing strategists work closely together to ensure that every detail of your book is a clear representation of the message in your writing.

**Want to know more?**
Write to us at info@publishyourgift.com
or call (888) 949-6228

Discover great books, exclusive offers, and more at
**www.PublishYourGift.com**

Connect with us on social media

@publishyourgift

www.ingramcontent.com/pod-product-compliance
Lightning Source LLC
Chambersburg PA
CBHW071529080526
44588CB00011B/1608